Copyright 2017, Rachelle Niemann
All rights reserved.
No part of this publication may be reproduced, distributed, or transmitted in any form or by any means, including photocopying, recording, or other electronic or mechanical methods, without the prior written permission of the publisher, except in the case of brief quotations embodied in reviews and certain other noncommercial uses permitted by copyright law.

grandoutdooradventures.com
rachelleniemann.com

Seek adventure in all you do.

Hastings, Minnesota

"An early morning walk is a blessing for the whole day."
- Henry David Thoreau

Just Breathe... And Breathe Again...

Hastings, Minnesota

"Afoot and lighthearted I take to the open road, healthy, free, the world before me."
- Walt Whitman

"Adventure is worthwhile in itself."
- Amelia Earhart

The Wave, Arizona

"One learns that the world, though made, is still being made."
– John Muir

"A journey of a thousand miles must begin with a single step."
– Lao Tzu

Elba, Minnesota

"Nobody trips over mountains. It is the small pebble that causes you to stumble. Pass all the pebbles in your path and you will find you have crossed the mountain."
- Unknown

Duluth, Minnesota

Elba, Minnesota

"And the day came when the risk to remain tight in a bud was more painful than the risk it took to blossom."
- Elizabeth Appell

"Love the life you have while you create the life of your dreams.
Don't think you have to choose one over the other."
- Hal Elrod

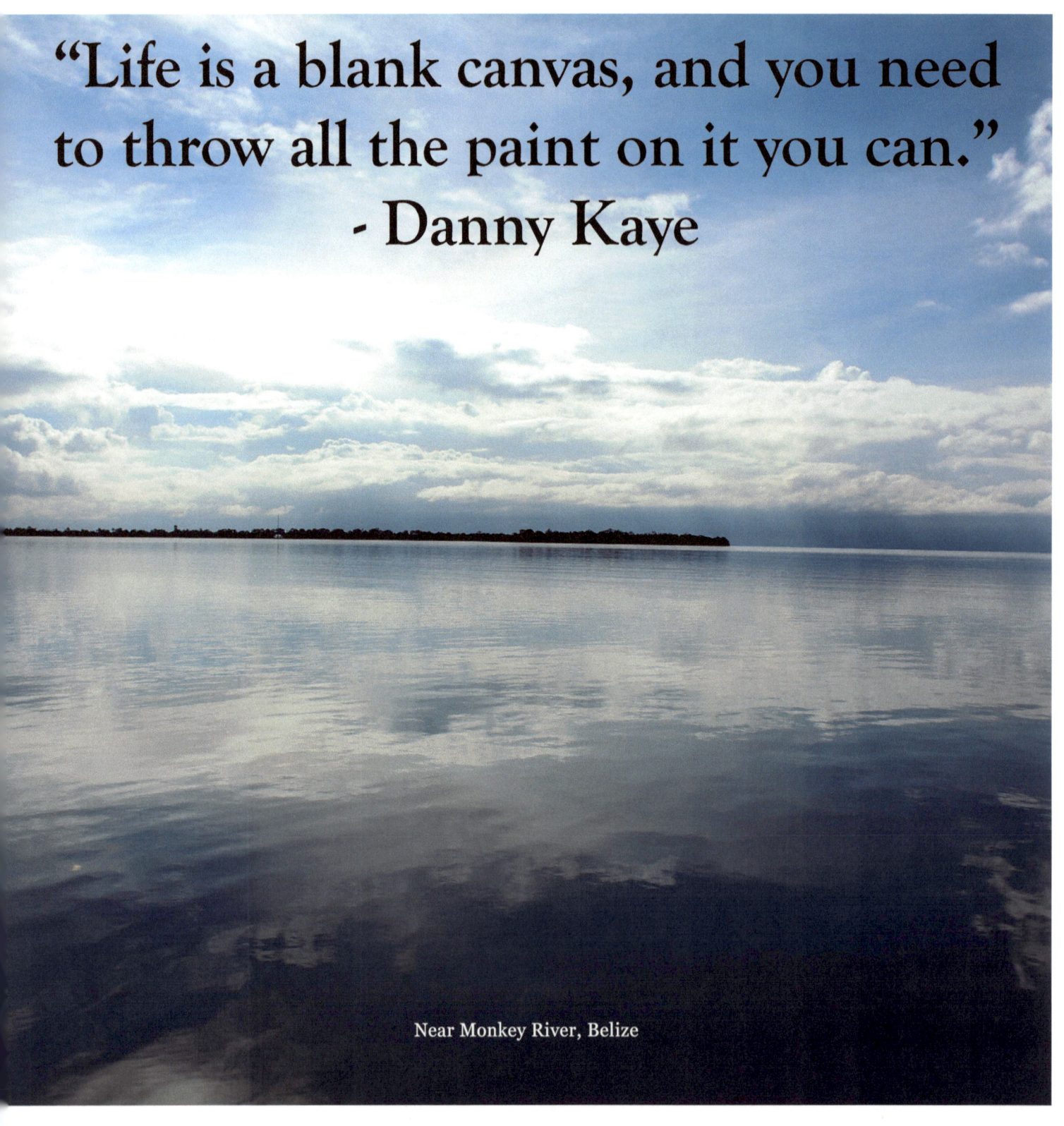

Near Monkey River, Belize

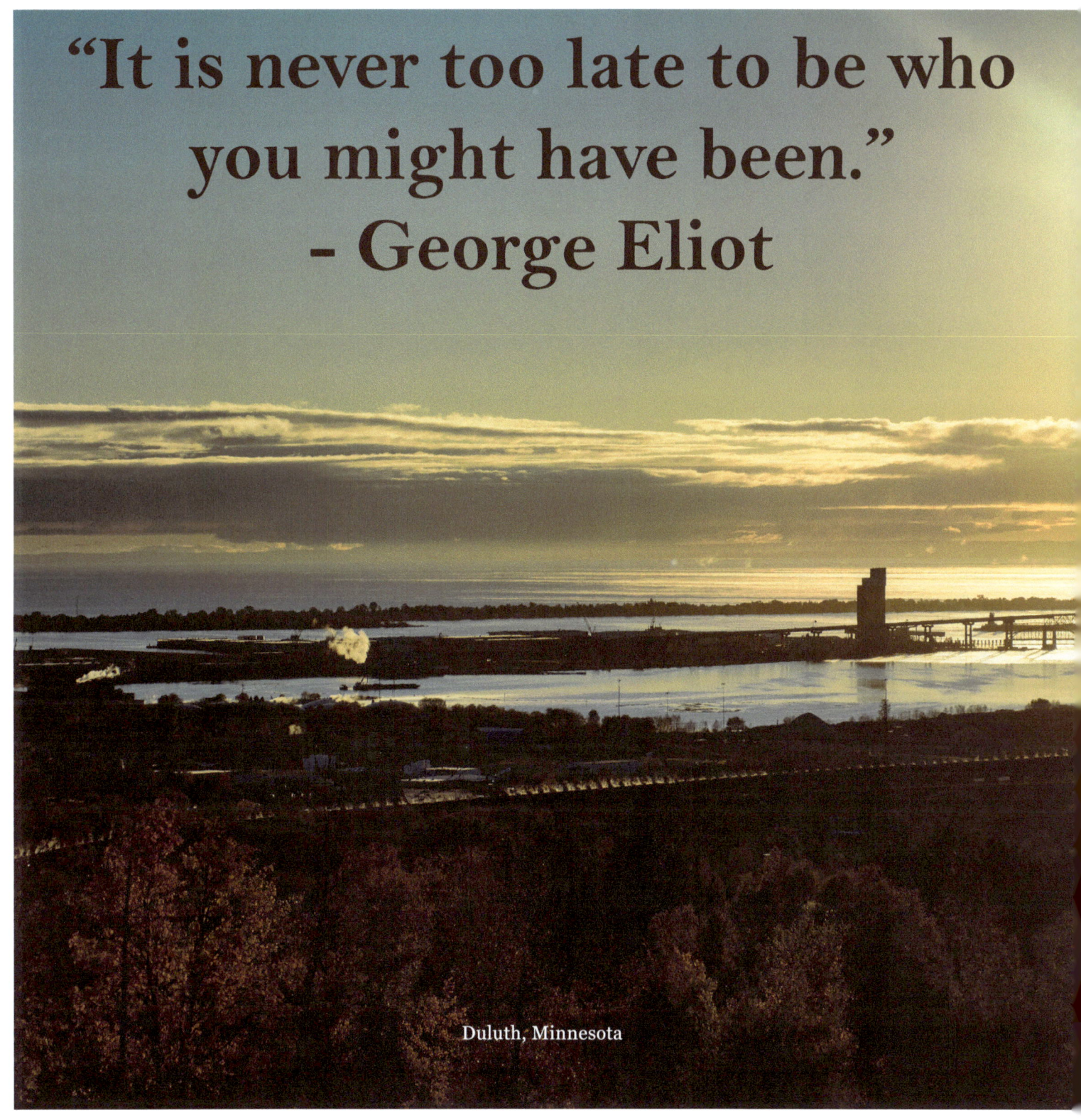

Burnsville, Minnesota

"There are always flowers for those who want to see them."
- Henri Matisse

"*Wherever you go, go with all your heart.*"
- Confucius

Moab, Utah

"Never underestimate the difference you can make."
~ Dan Casetta

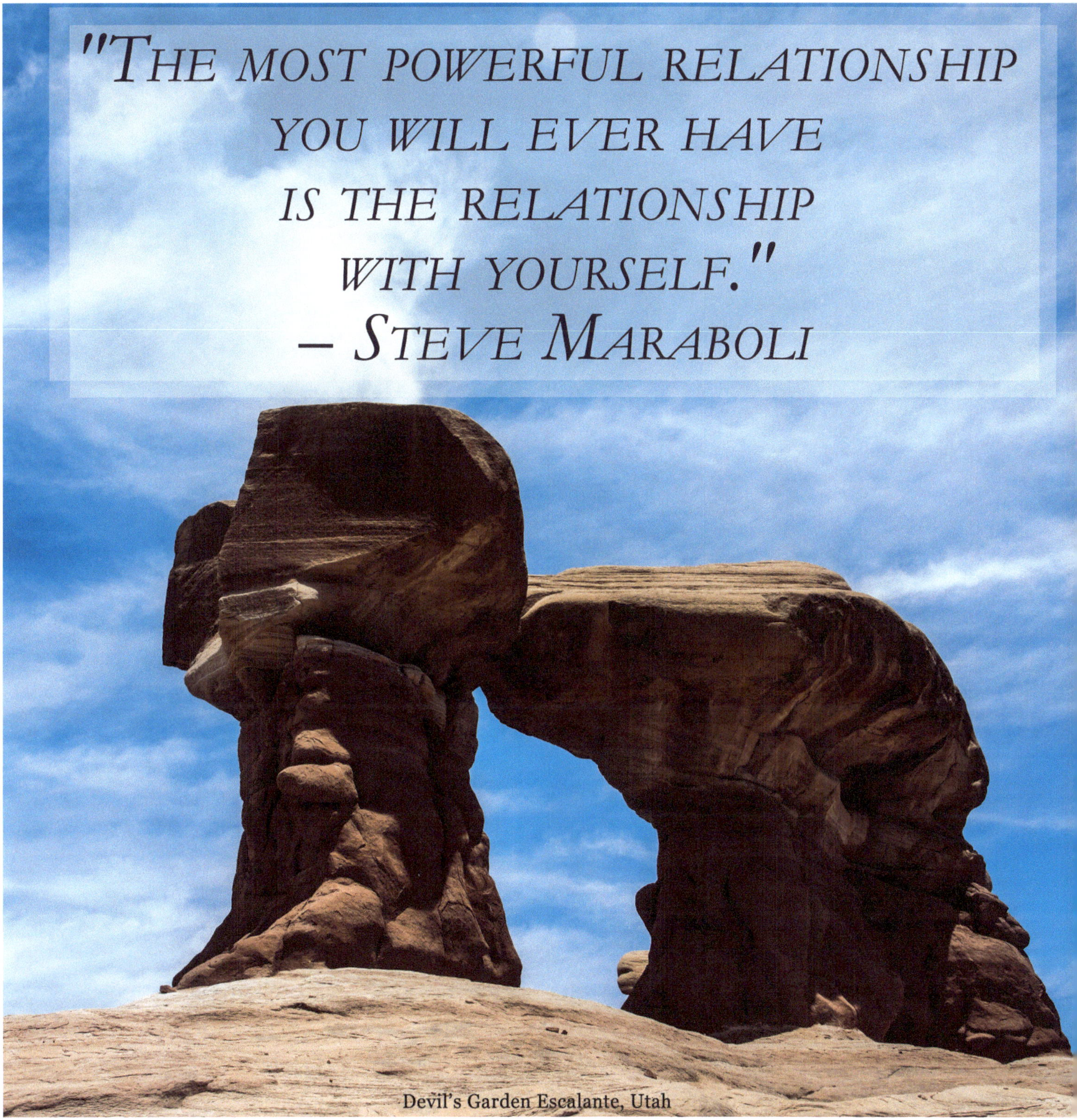

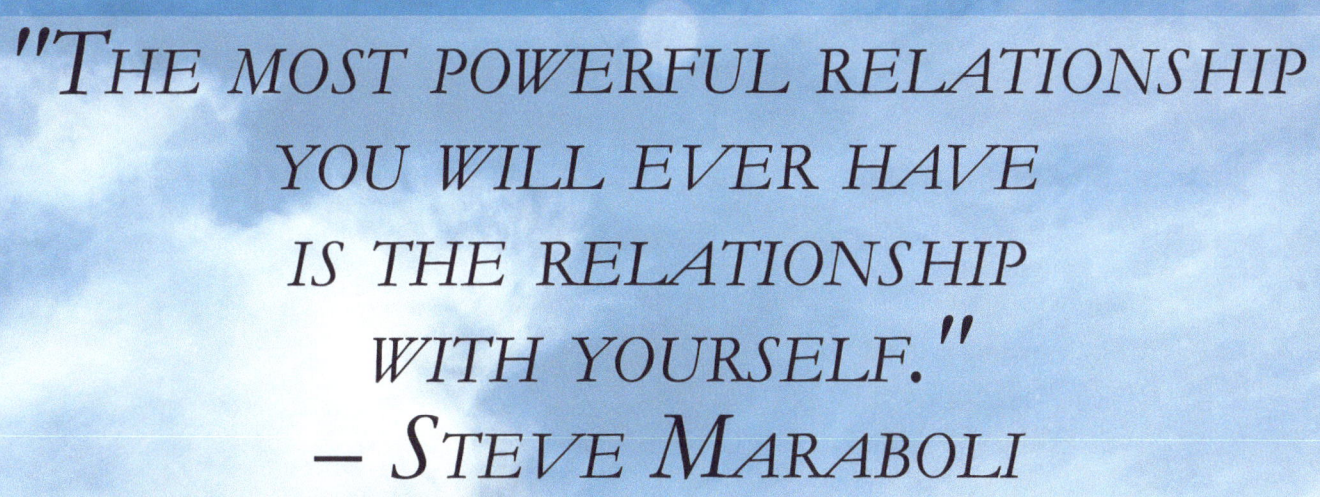

"The most powerful relationship you will ever have is the relationship with yourself."
— Steve Maraboli

Devil's Garden Escalante, Utah

Burnsville, Minnesota

Because beauty...
Take notice and appreciate...

Burnsville, Minnesota

"Your breathing is your greatest friend.
Return to it in all your troubles,
and you will find comfort and guidance."
- Unknown

Bequia

"Only those who risk going too far can possibly find out how far they can go."
- T.S. Eliot

Baja California, Mexico

"In any case you mustn't confuse a single failure with a final defeat."
- F. Scott Fitzgerald

Magdalena Bay, Baja California, Mexico

"Observe, record, tabulate, communicate. Use your five senses. Learn to see, learn to hear, learn to feel, learn to smell, and know that by practice alone you can become expert."
- William Osler

Angel's Landing, Zion NP, Utah

Fall in love with the journey over the outcome.

"Resilience is very different than being numb. Resilience means you experience, you feel, you fail, you hurt. You fall. But, you keep going."
- Yasmin Mogahed

Superstition Mountains, Arizona

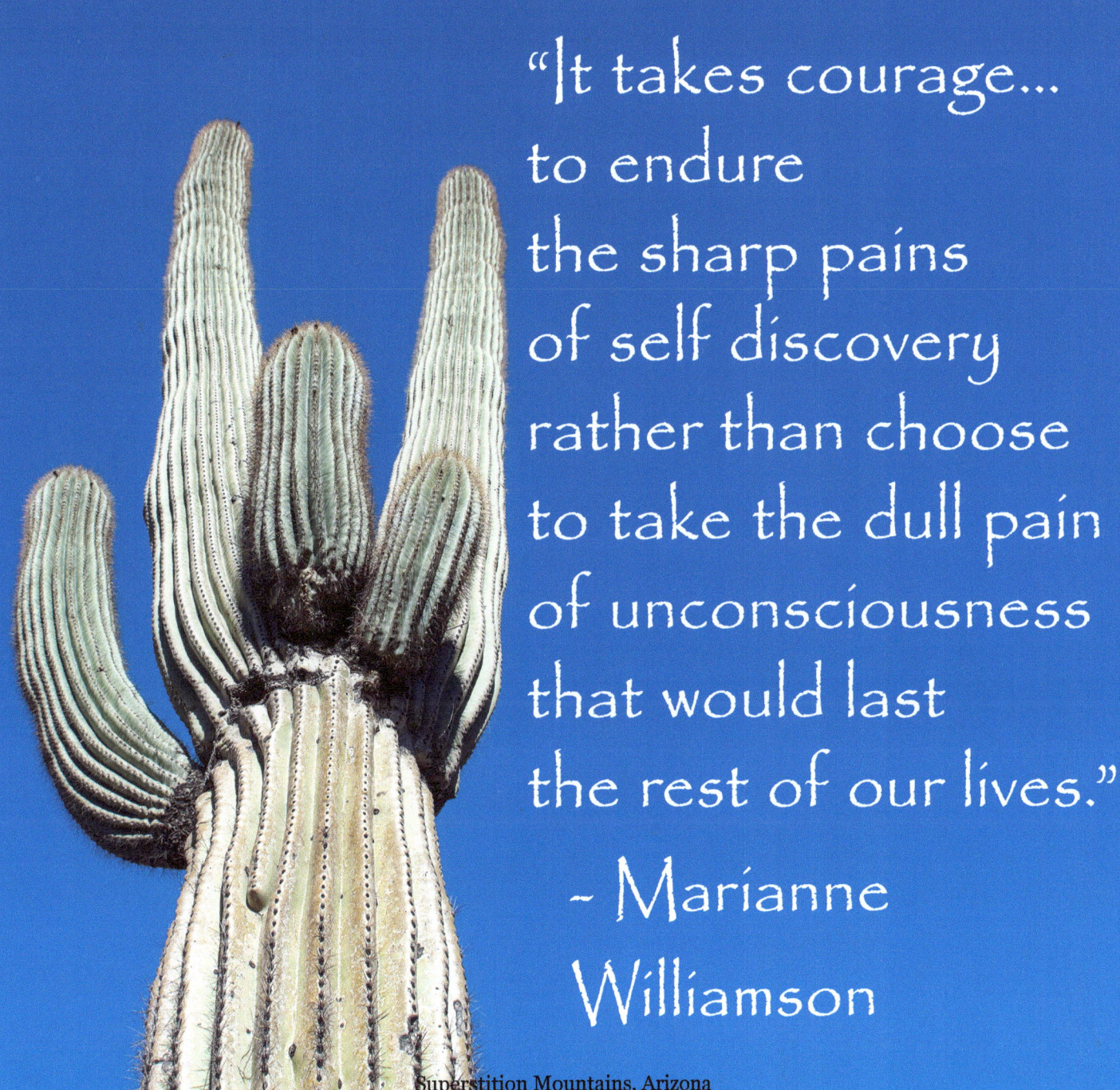

"Nourishing yourself in a way that helps you blossom in the direction you want to go is attainable,
and you are worth the effort."
~ Deborah Day

Zion National Park, Utah

"We keep moving forward, opening new doors, and doing new things, because we're curious and curiosity keeps leading us down new paths."
- Walt Disney

Minnesota

"Our task is not to seek for love, but merely to seek and find all the barriers within yourself that you have built against it."
~Rumi

San Francisco, California

"A river cuts through rock, not because of its power, but because of its persistence."
- Jim Watkins

Nankoweap Graineries, Grand Canyon, Arizona

"It is only in adventure that some people succeed in knowing themselves - in finding themselves."
- Andre Gide

Upper Antelope Canyon, Arizona

Two Harbors, Minnesota

"I haven't been everywhere, but it's on my list."
— Susan Sontag

Angel's Landing, Zion NP, Utah

"A man practices the art of adventure when he breaks the chain of routine and renews his life through reading new books, traveling to new places, making new friends, taking up new hobbies and adopting new viewpoints."
- Wilfred Peterson

Sometimes a break from routine is the very thing you need.

Elba, Minnesota

Upper Antelope Canyon, Arizona

"Pursue some path, however narrow and crooked, in which you can walk with love and reverence."
– Henry David Thoreau

Hastings, Minnesota

"Over every mountain there is a path, although it may not be seen from the valley."
- Theodore Roethke

"Keep close to Nature's heart...and break clear away, once in a while, and climb a mountain or spend a week in the woods. Wash your spirit clean."
- John Muir

Afton State Park, Minnesota

"The sun, with all those planets revolving around it and dependent upon it, can still ripen a bunch of grapes as if it had nothing else in the universe to do."
- Galileo

Duluth, Minnesota

"Autumn is a second spring when every leaf is a flower."
- Albert Camus

"Maybe my reliance on numbing is keeping me from the two things I was born for: Learning and Loving. I could go on hitting easy buttons until I die and feel no pain, but the cost of that decision could be that I'll never learn, love, or be truly alive."
- Glennon Melton Doyle

Duluth, Minnesota

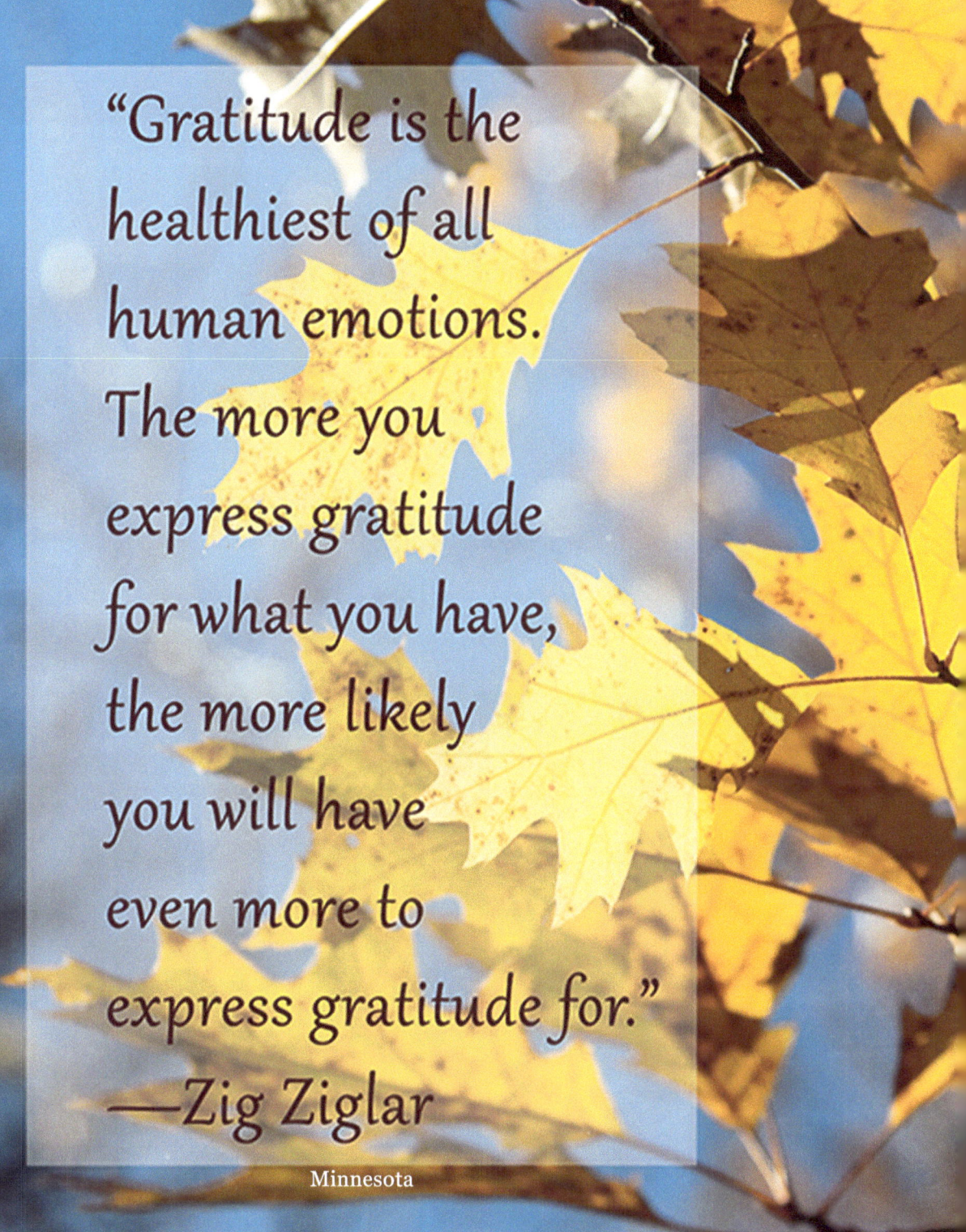

"Gratitude is the healthiest of all human emotions. The more you express gratitude for what you have, the more likely you will have even more to express gratitude for."
—Zig Ziglar

Minnesota

"As human beings one of our greatest gifts is the ability to choose our attitude in any given set of circumstances and to change the direction of our life."
- John Israel

Duluth, Minnesota

"Your attitude, not your aptitude,
will determine your altitude."
- Zig Ziglar

Grays Peak, Colorado

Gray's Peak, Colorado

"Even in our darkest winters, when things appear to be dead, seeds of opportunity are still alive."
- Jon Berghoff

"Only when we are brave enough to explore the darkness will we discover the infinite power of our light."
- Brene Brown

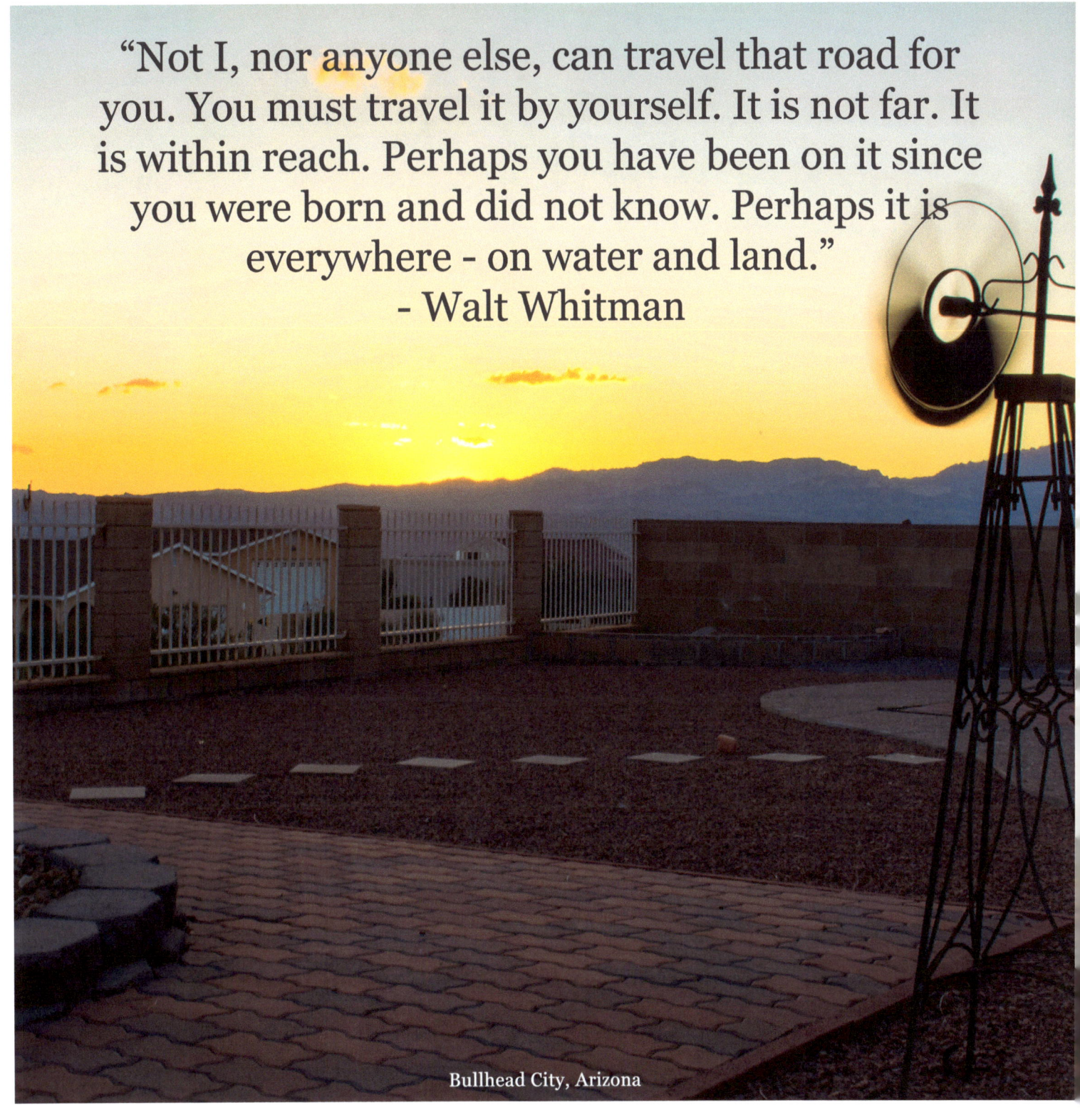

Florence, Oregon

"Wherever you go, no matter the weather, always bring your own sunshine."
- Anthony J. D'Angelo

The Moon

"You don't have to sit outside in the dark. If, however, you want to look at the stars, you will find that darkness is necessary. But the stars neither require nor demand it."
- Annie Dillard

www.ingramcontent.com/pod-product-compliance
Lightning Source LLC
Chambersburg PA
CBHW041119300426
44112CB00002B/28